W9-CFC-965

Italians love life and they love their work.

An Italian family that came from northern India.

The Director of Maintenance at a hotel.

Two shipyard repairmen.

An exchange student from Gambia in Africa.

A university student from Mestre.

A mother and son who own a hotel.

Two sailors from the Italian navy.

Two friends from Florence.

The postman brings good news.

Abdu from Dakar, Africa, sells purses in the piazza.

A craftsman makes religious objects for the tourists.

A Chinese father and son have an Italian restaurant.

A policeman and his friend in Sestri Levante.

Italians sometimes ride a bicycle all their lives.

ITALY
the people

Greg Nickles

A Bobbie Kalman Book

The Lands, Peoples, and Cultures Series

Crabtree Publishing Company

www.crabtreebooks.com

The Lands, Peoples, and Cultures Series

Created by Bobbie Kalman

Coordinating editor
Ellen Rodger

Production Coordinator
Rosie Gowsell

Project development, photo research, and design
First Folio Resource Group, Inc.
  Erinn Banting
  Pauline Beggs
  Tom Dart
  Bruce Krever
  Debbie Smith

Editing
Maggie MacDonald

Separations and film
Embassy Graphics

Printer
Worzalla Publishing Company

Consultants
Patricia Bucciero, Embassy of Italy–Ottawa; Carlo Settembrini, Italian Cultural Institute

Photographs
Mary Altier: p. 18 (top); Archive Photos/The Hulton-Getty Photo Collection: p. 6 (top), p. 7 (bottom), p. 10 (both); Archive Photos/Popperfoto: p. 21 (bottom); Martin Black/Impact: p. 14 (bottom), p. 30 (top); Robert Emmet Bright/Photo Researchers: p. 6 (bottom), p. 7 (top); Corbis/Tiziana and Gianni Baldizzone: p. 19 (right), p. 26 (bottom); Corbis/ Bettman: p. 11 (left); Corbis/Jonathan Blair: p. 15 (top); Corbis/Christel Gerstenberg: p. 24 (left); Corbis/Massimo Listri: p. 3; Corbis/Dennis Marsico: p. 23 (top); Corbis/Ted Spiegel: p. 22 (bottom); Corbis/Patrick Ward: p. 25 (top right); Corbis/ Michael S. Yamashita: cover, p. 20 (bottom); Peter Crabtree: front endpapers, back endpapers, title page, p. 4 (both), p. 12 (top), p. 13 (both), p. 14 (top), p. 15 (bottom), p. 16 (left), p. 17 (top), p. 18 (bottom), p. 19 (left), p. 20 (top), p. 23 (bottom), p. 25 (top left), p. 26 (top), p. 27 (top), p. 29 (right), p. 30 (bottom); Mario De Biasi/ Digital Stock: p. 5 (bottom); Chad Ehlers/ International Stock: p. 12 (bottom); Paul Forster/ Impact: p. 31; Giraudon/Art Resource: p. 8 (bottom); Beryl Goldberg: p. 21 (top); Grantpix/Photo Researchers: p. 22 (top); Christian Grzimek/Photo Researchers: p. 11 (right); Wolfgang Kaehler: p. 3, p. 5 (top), p. 16 (right); Andy Levin/ Photo Researchers: p. 17 (bottom); Magma Photos/ Balza/G. Neri: p. 24 (right); Richard T. Nowitz: p. 27 (bottom), p. 28, p. 29 (left); Brian Rybolt/Impact: p. 25 (bottom); Scala/Art Resource: p. 8 (top), p. 9 (both)

Illustrations
Dianne Eastman: icon
David Wysotski, Allure Illustrations: back cover

Cover: A gondola carries a bride and groom to their wedding reception at a café in Venice.

Title page: Two friends stop to chat during a bike ride in Parma, a city in northern Italy.

Icon: In Italy, soccer is called *calcio*. A *calcio* ball appears at the head of each section.

Back cover: The golden eagle lives in the Alps, a mountain range in the north of Italy.

Published by
Crabtree Publishing Company

PMB 16A
350 Fifth Avenue
Suite 3308
New York
NY 10118

612 Welland Avenue
St. Catharines
Ontario, Canada
L2M 5V6

73 Lime Walk
Headington
Oxford OX3 7AD
United Kingdom

Cataloging-in-Publication Data
Nickles, Greg, 1969–
Italy, the people / Greg Nickles.
p. cm. -- (The lands, peoples, and cultures series)
Includes index.
ISBN 0-7787-9370-2 (RLB) -- ISBN 0-7787-9738-4 (pbk.)
1. Italy--Social life and customs--Juvenile literature.
2. National characteristics, Italian.
[1. Italy--Social life and customs.]
I. Title. II. Series
DG441.N58 2001
945--dc21
                                    00-057074
                                    LC

Contents

A proud people

Two thousand years ago, the **ancestors** of the Italian people ruled a powerful **empire** from the city of Rome. According to an ancient legend, Rome was founded by mighty Romulus, son of the ancient god Mars. Romulus and his twin brother, Remus, were taken at birth by an evil king. The king wanted to drown them in the Tiber River. The strong twins survived. Years later, they defeated the king and founded a city on the spot where they were saved as infants. Romulus named the city "Rome," after himself, and became its first king.

Two people walk their dog through the old streets of Parma, in northern Italy.

A barbershop is both a place to get a haircut and a place to catch up on the latest gossip.

In the Piazza San Marco, in Venice, a mother and daughter let pigeons eat out of their hands.

A woman breaks the stems off hot peppers which she will use to make pasta sauce.

A magnificent past

Italians are proud of the part that Rome and the rest of their country has played in history. In addition to being the center of the ancient Roman Empire, their land later became home to the powerful Roman Catholic Church. In the centuries that followed, some of the world's brightest scholars, scientists, artists, and writers came from Italy.

Enjoying life

Today's Italians treasure the beautiful artwork, parks, and buildings that fill their towns and cities. They relax in their country's majestic mountains and on its sandy beaches. They spend long hours eating delicious meals and talking with friends and family. They also work hard for a future of which they can be proud.

Ancient Italy

People have lived on Italy's soil for thousands of years. The Etruscans, who built their cities about 2,600 years ago, were one of the first peoples in the north. Around the same time, settlers from Greece lived in Italy's south.

(top) In this painting, a crowd cheers for Romulus, the founder and first king of Rome.

(below) A wall painting in an Etruscan tomb shows people playing instruments, including a recorder and a harp.

The rise of Rome

Of all the cities ruled by the Etruscans, Rome became the strongest. In 510 B.C., the Romans decided that they wanted their independence. They began to compete with their former rulers for land and trade. By 400 B.C., the powerful Roman army controlled all the former Etruscan lands. By 270 B.C., it defeated the Greeks in the south and began invading other lands around the Mediterranean Sea.

The Roman Empire

At first, Rome was led by politicians elected by the **nobility** and the army. This changed in 48 B.C., when General Julius Caesar used military force to become leader. After his death, his nephew Caesar Augustus named himself **emperor**. For the next five centuries, Augustus and the emperors who came after him made the Roman Empire one of the greatest empires in history. At one point, its lands stretched all the way north to the British Isles and all the way south to the Middle East and Africa.

Caesar Augustus, shown in this sculpture, created a law called the Pax Romana. According to this law, any conquered nations could rule themselves as long as they paid taxes to the Roman Empire and fought in the Roman army.

Gladiators salute the emperor at the Circus Maximus, an arena in ancient Rome where public performances and gladiator fights were held.

Building the Empire

The Romans designed new towns and cities, and constructed paved roads. They built aqueducts, or bridge-like channels, to bring citizens fresh water. In each place they conquered, they spread their language, called Latin, their **culture**, and their laws.

Rulers and slaves

The people who ran the Roman Empire, including the emperor, generals, and politicians, lived in beautiful homes and enjoyed the best food, clothing, and entertainment. They were served by slaves. Many of these slaves were captured by Roman soldiers during battles in other lands. Unlike the rulers, the slaves lived in terrible conditions.

Roman pastimes

Romans had many pastimes. They loved to watch plays and dances at open-air stages called amphitheaters. They took hot saunas and baths at large public bathing houses. Many also went to stadiums such as the Colosseum in Rome to watch slaves, called gladiators, fight each other or wild animals to the death. Sometimes, helpless prisoners were thrown to hungry lions while the audience cheered. At other times, the Colosseum was flooded with water, and boats were used for fierce water battles.

Struggle and rebirth

Christianity began in the first century, during the time of the Roman Empire. Christianity is a religion based on the teachings of Jesus Christ, who is believed to be God's son on earth. Over the next four centuries, Rome became a center of Christianity. People who followed Rome's Christian Church were called Roman Catholics. The pope, the leader of the Roman Catholic Church, became very powerful. At his command, people were imprisoned, kings were named, and wars were started or stopped.

In this painting, a Roman Catholic priest baptizes Constantine I, the first Roman emperor to become a Christian.

Troubled times

The Roman Empire lasted until 476 A.D. By that time, many warring peoples, including the Goths, Vandals, Franks, and Lombards, had taken over the Empire's territory in Europe. Italy, too, was divided between these peoples into many small kingdoms. Centuries of war followed the end of the Roman Empire. Roman settlements fell into ruin, trade died off, and the ancient arts and sciences were mostly forgotten. As people in each kingdom developed their own language, Latin was no longer spoken throughout the land.

Powerful cities

By the year 1000, after centuries of war and struggle, cities such as Florence, Venice, Milan, and Naples became wealthy by trading spices, fabrics, and other goods with faraway lands. These cities did not belong to any kingdom. Instead, they ruled themselves and had their own armies. Prosperity ended around 1350, when a terrible disease called the Black Death killed one-third of all Italians. It took decades before the cities returned to their former glory.

Marco Polo (1254–1324)

Marco Polo was from Venice. He was one of the first Europeans to travel to Asia's Far East. Born to a family of **merchants**, the young Marco began his first long voyage with his father and uncle in 1271. They took about four years to travel to China. There, they visited the emperor, Kublai Khan, and toured his kingdom for many years.

In 1295, after 24 years, the Polos finally returned home with silk, jewels, and other riches given to them by the Khan. They had been gone from Venice so long that their friends and relatives thought they had died. Later explorers who read of Polo's travels, including the Italian explorer Cristoforo Colombo, also known as Christopher Columbus, were inspired to find new trade routes to the Far East where they, too, could find riches.

Filipo Brunelleschi, an architect during the Renaissance, shows a model for a building to Cosimo De Medici.

The rebirth

For centuries, some of Europe's most talented scholars and artists had worked for the Roman Catholic Church. As Italy's cities became more powerful, their rulers and wealthy families, such as the De Medici of Florence, also hired these talented people. The scholars and artists started to study the ideas of the ancient Roman Empire. By the 1400s, they had rediscovered Roman sculpture, architecture, and mathematics. They were also making new discoveries. The next 200 years was a period known as the *Rinascimento*, or Renaissance. Renaissance means "rebirth." During this time, people in Italy led Europe in the arts and sciences.

War and rebellion

By the 1600s, powerful kingdoms in other parts of Europe had captured much of Italy. The region was weakened even more by religious wars that began when Christians called Protestants split away from the Roman Catholic Church. The pope lost the vast powers that he once had.

By the 1800s, many Italians had become unhappy with their kings and with other foreign rulers. They wanted to elect their own leaders. Some joined the *Risorgimento* movement. This movement fought to combine the land's many kingdoms into a single, united country. It led many bloody **rebellions** that were unsuccessful.

Galileo Galilei (1564–1642)

Galileo Galilei was one of Italy's most brilliant scientists. He specialized in mathematics and astronomy, or the study of the stars and planets. Using a new invention, the telescope, Galileo discovered that the sun was the center of the solar system. This idea went against the view of the Roman Catholic Church. At that time, the Church taught that the sun and other planets revolved around the earth. Galileo was arrested by the Church because of his beliefs. In 1633, he was sentenced to spend the rest of his life imprisoned in his home.

Giuseppe Garibaldi calls to his troops after a battle against the French in Rome. The French, under the rule of Napoleon, controlled most of Italy's land before Garibaldi's success in uniting Italy.

In this painting from 1870, Italian troops move across a battlefield in Rome during the final phase of Italian unification.

By 1850, King Vittorio Emanuele II of Piedmont and Sicily allowed his subjects to elect some of their leaders. With his talented general, Giuseppe Garibaldi, and prime minister, Camillo Benso di Cavour, this popular king began fighting to take over the rest of the land. After several battles, people in other kingdoms voted to join Vittorio Emanuele II. By 1861, he became king of a newly united country called Italy. Within the next ten years, the last pieces of Italy, Venice and Rome, also joined the country.

Mussolini and fascism

Italy was a country at last, but the battles that united it had hurt its people and economy. Millions of people were poor, especially in the countryside. Conditions were so bad that many moved to other countries such as the United States, Canada, Australia, Argentina, and Brazil. The problems became worse after World War I (1914–1918), during which hundreds of thousands of Italians died.

Italians disagreed on how to solve their problems. The politician Benito Mussolini, who became leader in 1922, thought that he could unite all Italians and improve the country with his fascist ideas. Fascist leaders believe in having a strong army and a powerful central government which controls the economy. They often have very **patriotic** views. They do not believe in elections or allow free speech. When fascist leaders become too powerful, they use their soldiers and police to force people to obey their commands.

Mussolini addresses Italian soldiers from the top of a tank during World War II.

Into battle

Mussolini introduced modern factories, farming, and transportation, which helped Italy. He also brought in special programs to help children and people who were no longer working. Promising a new Roman Empire, he led the country into wars in Spain and Ethiopia in the 1930s. He took Italy into World War II in 1939, fighting on the side of Germany. By 1945, Germany and its **allies** had been defeated. The Italians **executed** Mussolini and, in the next year, set up a government elected by the people.

Organized crime

Italy went through decades of war, **revolution**, and corruption throughout the 1800s and 1900s. Without law and order, families of gangsters organized into the powerful *Mafiosi*, or Mafia. The *Mafiosi* are involved in many illegal businesses, including the drug trade, gambling, and loan sharking, or loaning money at very high interest rates. People have tried to bring the *Mafiosi* to justice, but the criminals are still fairly powerful, especially on the island of Sicily.

Building a new Italy

The destruction caused by the war led many more Italians to move overseas. Those who remained faced the difficult job of rebuilding their country. Other countries, especially the United States, gave billions of dollars in aid. By the late 1950s, businesses thrived. Italy had some of the world's most modern, productive factories.

Despite the success of Italy's economy, its government has had several setbacks since 1945. There are so many political parties that it is difficult for any one party to win an election. As well, many politicians have been found guilty of **corruption**, including accepting **bribes** and helping criminals. As a result, Italy's regions and cities have formed strong governments to solve local problems.

The Galleria Vittorio Emanuele II was built in honor of the first king of the united Italy. It was almost completely destroyed by bombs during World War II, but has since been restored and rebuilt into a modern shopping center.

 # The Italian people

Some of today's Italians are **descendants** of Etruscans and Greeks who settled in the region thousands of years ago. Others have ancestors who invaded the land in the last 1,500 years. Still others are related to people in neighboring countries or are recent **immigrants** to Italy.

The same but different

About 98 percent of Italians have traditions, holidays, and religious beliefs that are very much alike. There are some differences, however, between people who live in different regions. These differences stem from the time when Italy was separated into many kingdoms. People in each kingdom developed their own traditions, festivals, and dialects, or versions, of Italian. Even today, many people feel more closely connected to their region than to Italy as a whole.

(above) A woman rests on a bench in front of a pile of wood in a small village. The wood will be used to heat people's homes.

(top) A mother holds her son while he rides on a merry-go-round.

12

A father and daughter run an antique shop that sells paintings, lamps, and furniture.

Sardinians

Italians on the island of Sardinia have a culture that reflects the fact that they are quite far from mainland Italy. Many different peoples have ruled the island. They include the Sards, a Mediterranean people after whom the island was named; the Islamic Saracens from Africa, who spoke Arabic; and the Spanish. Today, Sardinia's population of over 1.5 million speaks different dialects of Italian as well as some Spanish, Arabic, and the local language, Sardo.

Along the border

Hundreds of thousands of people in Italy's far north have languages and cultures that are closely related to those of people in countries that border Italy. The largest of these groups, the German-Italians, speak Ladin, a dialect influenced by German. They are closely related to their German-speaking neighbors in Austria. French-Italians live near Italy's border with France and Switzerland, where French is spoken. Slavic-Italians live close to the Slavic-speaking country of Slovenia.

New Italians

Italy is now home to many people who have recently arrived from other parts of the world. Most settle in the cities, where they work in Italy's industries. Thousands of **refugees** from the former Yugoslavia fled to Italy after wars in the early 1990s. Immigrants have also come from North Africa and the Middle East. Many are followers of Islam, the religion based on the teachings of the **prophet** Muhammad.

People talk, eat, drink coffee and relax in the sun at a café in Parma.

Italian families

Italian families are known for being extremely close-knit. Children, parents, grandparents, aunts, uncles, and cousins spend more time together than most people throughout Europe and North America. Relatives are so close that a common Italian expression says the family is "like a fortress."

One reason for these strong family ties is Italy's troubled history. With wars, corruption, and other problems, Italians learned they could not always rely on their leaders to look out for them. Instead, family members had to protect one another from harm. They also had to make sure their relatives were fed, clothed, housed, and had jobs.

Families past and present

Until the last half of the 1900s, most Italian families were large, but they had small homes and very little money. Extended families lived in the same house. Today, relatives are still close to one another, but families are smaller. Usually, just one or two children and their parents live together. Young children are especially close with their grandparents, who often take care of them while their parents are at work.

Around the table

Italian family gatherings are fun events with lots of food, wine, and conversation. Sunday afternoon is one of the most popular times to get together. Family members meet for a huge meal in a relative's house, local café, or restaurant. In warm weather, the get-togethers often take place outside.

(left) After supper, many Italian families take a **passegiata**, *or stroll, together.*

(below) A family enjoys a picnic of bread, vegetables, fruit, and wine in the hills of Tuscany, a region in western Italy.

Children carrying lilies and baptismal candles leave a Roman Catholic church after their first communion.

A bride and groom pose for pictures after their wedding at the city hall.

Childhood ceremonies

Some of the most important family events in Italians' lives are special religious ceremonies that welcome young people into the Roman Catholic Church. Traditionally, **baptisms**, **first communions**, and **confirmations** were celebrated with family parades through the streets. Today, there are large parties.

Wedding bells

One of the most joyous family celebrations is a wedding. Relatives from near and far attend the ceremony, which usually takes place in a church. Guests offer their *tanti auguri*, or "best wishes," to the couple and throw rice or *confetti*, a traditional candy made of white sugar-coated almonds. The bride and groom might also give small bags of *confetti* to guests as *bomboniere*, or reminders of the celebration. At the party following the ceremony, people enjoy a delicious meal and dance.

Italian cities are full of action and interesting sights. Scooters and cars jam the streets, and pedestrians crowd the sidewalks. Impressive office towers and beautiful old buildings line the downtown section, while large homes, apartment buildings, and department stores are spread throughout the **suburbs**.

Visiting the streets

Streets in the downtown sections of Italy's cities are very narrow. They were built centuries ago for pedestrians, horses, and small carriages. These means of transportation did not need as much room as cars, which had not been invented yet!

Along the narrow streets are old shops, restaurants, apartments, and other buildings. There are also ruins that date back to the ancient Roman Empire. At the center of the city is a *piazza*, or main square, where the city's **cathedral** and government buildings are found. The suburbs are less busy than downtown, with streets that are newer and wider.

Apartment buildings line a narrow canal in Venice. People travel through Venice by boat or by foot, crossing the many bridges that span the canals.

City homes

Downtown, most people live in small apartments, in stone buildings that are only a few stories high. Some of these buildings are hundreds of years old and were built around a courtyard. In the newer suburbs, people live in tall, concrete apartment buildings or in single-family homes. These houses have a garage and yard, and look much like those in North American suburbs.

Apartment buildings, homes, and gardens crowd a neighborhood in Florence.

The work day

Most Italians in cities work in offices, factories, or service industries such as banking or teaching. Their work day begins around eight o'clock in the morning. The lunch break is around noon. Traditionally, people went home for lunch, taking a three-hour break during the hottest time of the day. Sometimes, they even took a short nap called a *pennichella*. Then, they went back to work until seven o'clock in the evening. Today, more Italians in cities take short lunches and leave work around five o'clock.

Grocery shopping

Large supermarkets are becoming popular in the suburbs, but most Italians still prefer to buy fresh food each day at neighborhood shops and outdoor markets. Each local shop specializes in a different food such as smoked meat, cheese and other dairy products, bread, and fruit and vegetables.

Lines of laundry, strung from apartment windows, are a common sight above city streets in Perugia.

At his vegetable stand, a local vendor fills a bag with basil, an herb used in many Italian dishes.

17

Italy's small towns and villages are scattered across the countryside. Some are perched on rocky hilltops. Others stand amid vast fields of farmland or along the seacoast.

People who live in the countryside work hard, but their daily lives are more peaceful than those of city dwellers. Their narrow streets are quiet because there are few cars. There is less pollution and much less crowding. Unlike in cities, where neighbors often do not know one another, country people often know everyone in their community.

Changing times

Years ago, most Italians lived in the countryside. They had little money, their small houses and apartments were crowded, and they often had no electricity or running water. Millions of people moved to the cities in search of a better life. Since then, the government constructed new homes, roads, schools, and hospitals in the countryside. It built **dams** and **reservoirs** to provide a source of water, helped pay for indoor plumbing and electricity, and helped farmers buy tractors and other equipment. Today, about a third of all Italians live in the countryside.

A family grows onions, lettuce, and different types of herbs in a small garden outside their home in the Alps.

An old farmhouse and farm buildings sit on a hill amid the rolling hills of Tuscany.

Students gather in the main **piazza** *of San Gimignano, a small medieval town in Tuscany.*

Towns and villages

Even with newer buildings and modern conveniences, many Italian towns and villages look much the same as they did centuries ago. Their streets are paved with stones and lined with buildings from centuries past. Fortress walls still surround some towns, built at a time when the townspeople had to protect themselves against enemies.

Town life centers around the small *piazza*. The *piazza* is surrounded by a church, the town hall, several shops, and a café. As in the city, the *piazza* is a favorite spot for friends and families to meet and catch up on the latest news or for people who just want to read a newspaper or watch people going by.

Country homes

Traditional country homes usually have whitewashed stone walls and roofs covered in bumpy tiles. Farmhouses are often tiny cottages, but some have two floors. The bottom floor is for **livestock** and the top floor is for people. In towns, people live in two- or three-story houses that each have several apartments or in new, concrete apartment buildings.

Many rural families in the southern hills once lived in homes made from caves. Today, these caves are used mostly to house livestock. People still live in traditional *trulli* homes, however. These old, round houses with cone-shaped roofs are found in the southern region of Apulia.

Farm life

Some people in towns and villages work in small shops. Others are artisans who make tools and crafts. Most people in the countryside, however, work on farms like their ancestors. The entire family, from children to grandparents, helps with the chores. They begin work at dawn and finish at sunset, with a break in the middle of the day. During this break, they eat their main meal and take a nap.

The harvest is the busiest time of the year. At times, it is so busy that farmers hire extra help to bring in their crops. After the harvest, there are huge celebrations where everyone enjoys the first fresh foods of the season.

Cows graze in an enclosure outside a rural home in Piedmont, in northwest Italy.

 # At school

In many ways, school in Italy is much like school in North America. Children attend both elementary and high schools. They study subjects such as science, languages, math, music, history, and religion. Many students continue their education at college or university.

A typical day

In most of Italy, students have classes six days a week. Classes begin around eight-thirty in the morning and end around one o'clock in the afternoon. There are few after-school activities, so after lunch children do their homework, chores, or play soccer and other games with friends. In some places, school lasts all day. Students eat lunch, do crafts, and play sports in the afternoon.

(right) Younger children sometimes wear simple school uniforms that look like smocks.

(top) After classes, students wait for their friends outside their high school.

Students run and play in the Piazza del Nettuno during a field trip in Bologna.

School years

Some Italian children go to kindergarten, called *scuola materna*, when they are three, four, or five years old. Everyone must begin elementary school at the age of six. After five years, students go to junior high, called *scuola media*, which lasts three years. A favorite part of *scuola media* are field trips to some of Italy's most famous historical sites, museums, and art galleries. Some of these places are just around the corner, but others are a two- or three-day trip away.

Higher grades

All students in Italy must complete a difficult exam to graduate from junior to senior high school. If they pass, they can choose which kind of senior high school they will attend. Some students go to a vocational school to learn a **trade**. Others attend a *magistero* to become a teacher. Those who wish to study later at university attend a *liceo*, a school that teaches subjects such as sciences, arts, and languages. After five years, all students must write another difficult exam, called the *maturità*, to receive their high school diploma. They study weeks for the *maturità* and wait nervously for their marks. Students hope they score well because their results are printed in the newspaper!

The Montessori method

Dr. Maria Montessori is one of the most famous educators in the world. In 1894, after becoming the first woman in Italy to earn a medical degree, she began studying how children were taught. Montessori believed that schools were too competitive. They did not let students explore their own talents and ideas. In 1907, she opened her own school, encouraging her students to be curious and learn at their own speed. Her approach was so successful that she opened several more schools and began training new teachers in the Montessori method. By the time she died in 1952, she had changed the way children were taught around the world.

Italians love outdoor sports and games such as soccer and *bocce*, a kind of bowling played with wooden balls. Indoor games, including cards and *tombola*, a type of bingo that uses 90 numbers instead of 70, are also popular.

*(top) In **bocce**, two teams compete to roll their balls closest to a target ball called a **pallino**.*

*(below) Players struggle to get the ball away from one another at a **Calcio Fiorentino** game. The ball is made of cowhide and is very heavy.*

Soccermania!

Like many people around the world, Italians love soccer, which they call *calcio*. Italians around the globe watch the national *calcio* team. Every game is an excuse for street parties and flag-waving. Crowds cheer as the players "head" the ball in mid-flight, dribble it along as they run, and shoot it past the goalie to score.

Italian children learn to play *calcio* when they are very young. Practically every neighborhood, town, city, and region has a team. Large playing fields are built even in the smallest villages, and bright lights are installed so that teams can compete after dusk.

Soccer in Florence

Each year, the city of Florence hosts a wild soccer game called *Calcio Fiorentino*, or "Florentine Soccer." It is part of the celebration for Saint John the Baptist, a religious figure who is honored in many countries on June 24. Florence's 500-year-old Santa Croce *piazza* is covered with sand and transformed into a soccer field for the occasion. Four teams of 27 players each, dressed in **medieval** costume, compete for the prize of a white calf.

Spectators by the side of a road watch cyclists speed past during a race in Sicily.

The great Italian outdoors

The nearby Alps and Apennines are favorite mountains for skiers, hikers, and rock-climbers. Swimmers and people who like to sail enjoy Italy's oceans and lakes. Annual bicycle and car races draw huge crowds of onlookers. Cyclists compete in the grueling *Giro d'Italia* race. It covers 1,700 miles (2,750 kilometers), including many steep mountain roads. The Italian Grand Prix, held near Milan, is the most famous car race. Another famous race is the *Mille Miglia*, or "Thousand Mile" event. During the *Mille Miglia*, race cars speed along the same roads that regular cars, buses, scooters, and bikes are traveling.

Card games

Card games, whether played indoors or in the local park or *piazza*, are popular with Italians of all ages. Many of these games, such as *scopa* and *briscola*, are played with an "Italian" or "Naples" deck. This deck is made up of 40 cards in four suits: swords, sticks, cups, and coins. Several other decks, including the 52-card deck familiar to North Americans, are also used in Italy.

People gather in a piazza in Venice to watch two friends play a game of chess.

More and more *morra*

One of the simplest Italian games is also one of the most fun. *Morra* players need no equipment — just their hands. Play *morra* with a friend:

- Face your friend and hold out a fist.
- At the exact same time, you and your friend extend some of your fingers and call out a number from one to five. Neither you nor your friend can look at the other's hand as you call out the number.
- If the number you call matches the number of fingers your friend holds out, you win the round. If you both guess correctly or incorrectly, the round is a "draw."
- Try playing more and more quickly until you are both going as fast as you can.

Italian fashion

Italians are known for their sense of style. They try to dress their best even when they are just going for a stroll in their neighborhood. Italian fashion designers are known around the world. They create beautiful clothing, footwear, and **accessories** that are sold in some of the most expensive shops.

A tradition of fashion

Since ancient times, Italians have manufactured and traded rich fabrics. The leaders of the Roman Empire and, later, kings, popes, and wealthy families had their clothes made from the region's finest fabrics. Purple cloth was often reserved for Roman emperors and other top leaders because the dye used to make it was very rare and expensive. It came from shellfish.

A fashion center

Some of the world's most famous fashion houses are based in Italy. Armani designs suits. Gucci is famous for its shoes and handbags. Benetton makes sweaters and other knitwear. Milan is the center of Italy's fashion industry. Twice each year, the city hosts its *Collezione*, or "Collections," fashion shows. Fashion designers, models, photographers, and journalists from around the world attend these shows.

A model wears an outfit by Gianfranco Ferrè, a popular Italian designer, at a fashion show in Milan.

In this mosaic, Justinian the Great, an emperor from ancient Rome, wears a purple sash held together by a fancy pin.

(right) A woman wears a fancy costume at the feast of Saint Ephisio, a regional holiday on the island of Sardinia.

(below) Friends wear pants, shirts, and jackets on a cool spring day in Sestri Levante, in northwest Italy.

Everyday clothes and more

The type of clothing that Italians wear is the same as that worn by North Americans — pants, shirts, and dresses — but their clothing is more stylish. In the largest cities and in the smallest villages, people work hard so that they can afford designer clothes. Until 30 years ago, they rarely wore shorts, even when the weather was hot, because shorts were considered sportswear. Today, teens are starting to dress more casually, like North American teens.

The law of fashion

Even Italy's police officers and guards dress with style. *Carabineri* control demonstrations and crime. Their traditional uniforms, worn for show, include a three-cornered hat, a white sash and gloves, a dark blue cape lined in red, and a sword. Their usual uniforms are much less elaborate and change depending on the season. They wear dark green in the summer and black in the winter. *Corazzieri*, who guard Italy's president, wear glittering helmets with long feathers, dark coats with white pants, and tall boots.

*Two **carabineri**, dressed in uniform, stand in La Galleria, a shopping mall in Florence.*

A hotelowner makes **caffè** **latte** *for a customer.*

In Italy, mealtime is always a great pleasure. Most people begin their day with *caffè latte*, which is coffee with a little milk. They also eat a light roll or a flaky pastry called a *cornetto* or *brioche*. Children drink *latte è caffè*, which is milk with a little coffee. They put it in a bowl and add cookies or bread.

In some places, lunch is the main meal of the day. It is served around two in the afternoon. In other places, the late-evening supper is the main meal.

Courses of a meal

People often spend a long time preparing and eating their main meal. On special occasions, it may have up to eight courses. *Antipasti*, or appetizers, are served first. These are often bread with olive oil, cheese, or meats such as *prosciutto*, a type of ham. Soup or pasta follow, and then vegetables with meat or fish. Salad is served after the main course. The meal ends with dessert, which is often cheese or fruit and coffee.

A man slices bread, cheese, salami, and sausages for a family dinner.

A butcher sells cold meats and cheese at a local market in Florence.

Fine wine

Italy produces more wine than any other country. Young and old drink it with every main meal. It is produced both on small family-owned vineyards where the harvest is still done by hand and on huge estates where machines do most of the work. Both *rosso*, or red, and *bianco*, or white, wines are very popular.

Regional foods

Many regions in Italy have their own specialties. For example, pizza comes from Naples. The city of Parma is the home of hard, tangy Parmesan cheese and *prosciutto*. Tuscany, in the west, is known for its large beef steaks. They can weigh almost two pounds (one kilogram)!

Italian ingredients

Italian food would not taste the same without a few important ingredients. Garlic is a plant with a bulb that grows underground. Cooks break the bulb into cloves, or sections. They chop or crush the cloves to release the garlic's strong flavor and smell. Basil and oregano are much milder than garlic. They are herbs, or plants. Fresh basil leaves and dried oregano flowers are ground up and added to food as flavoring. Olives, olive oil, and tomatoes are also important in Italian cooking.

Fresh fruit, vegetables, and herbs are sold in markets all over Italy.

National pasta

Italy is known for pasta. A popular legend says that Marco Polo brought it from China in the 1200s. In fact, pasta has been made in Italy for thousands of years. Archaeologists, people who study the past by looking at buildings and artifacts, have even found artwork in ancient Etruscan tombs of people making pasta!

Most Italians like their pasta fresh. They mix water with semolina flour and sometimes egg to make a very sticky dough. The dough is put into a press, where it is squeezed into different shapes. It can also be rolled and cut in different widths and lengths. The pasta is then cooked and served with a favorite *ragù*, or tomato sauce, cheese, olive oil, or *pesto*, which is made from chopped basil leaves, ground pine nuts, and cheese.

Pasta name	Translation	Illustration
spaghetti	a length of cord	
radiatore	radiators	
farfalle	butterflies	
ruote	wheels	
tortellini	little cakes	
agnolotti	little fat lambs	

A chef rolls dough through a pasta machine, which he turns by hand. After the flat piece of dough comes through the machine, the chef cuts it into different shapes.

The home of pizza

Pizza was invented in Naples in the 1700s as a cheap meal. At first, it was sold from street stalls, called *pizzerie*. In 1889, a pizza was created in honor of Queen Margherita. It was made with dough, which is white; tomatoes, which are red; and basil, which is green. White, red, and green are the colors of Italy's flag. This pizza was called a Margherita. It was a hit and became popular outside of Naples. When Italians moved to other countries, they brought their recipes with them. Pizza quickly became a favorite meal in their new home.

Make your own pizza

It is easy to make pizza. All you need are a few ingredients and an adult's help.

Ingredients:
- 4 small pizza shells, available at grocery stores
- two cookie sheets
- a large spoon
- a can of tomato sauce
- basil, either dried or fresh and chopped
- 8 ounces (225 grams) mozzarella cheese, grated or broken into chunks
- olive oil (optional)
- an oven, preheated to 425° Fahrenheit (220° Celsius)

Instructions:
- Lay out the pizza shells on the cookie sheets.
- Use the spoon to spread the tomato sauce all over the shells. Be careful not to let it dribble over the sides.
- Sprinkle the shells with a little basil.
- Divide and sprinkle the cheese over the shells.
- Dribble a little olive oil over each pizza.
- Place the cookie sheets in the oven. Bake 10-15 minutes, or until the cheese begins to bubble and brown. Serve immediately.

Inventors of ice cream

In the 1800s, Italians invented recipes for the kinds of ice cream we enjoy today. Most *gelato*, or ice cream, is made by heating and mixing cream, sugar, and eggs. Some *gelato* is made with water instead of cream. It is like sherbet. Nuts, fruit, and other flavorings are added to the *gelato*, which is then frozen. The *gelato* must be mixed as it chills so that it does not freeze solid. *Granita*, ice water flavored with lemon juice or coffee, is also popular.

An ice cream parlor in Mestre, in northeastern Italy near Venice, sells many different flavors of gelato, including chocolate, strawberry, and lemon.

A boy puts tomato sauce, fresh basil, and mozzarella cheese on a pizza shell.

 # A trip to the country

Aldo frowned and looked out the window as *Mama* drove the car up the road that led to her parents' hillside village. It had been a long drive from their home in Florence. Aldo's father looked back at him. "You don't look happy," he said.

"This twisty road is making me sick, *Babbo*," Aldo grumbled. "And, I'm going to miss the *calcio* match between Italy and Argentina, unless *Nonno* and *Nonna* finally bought a TV."

Aldo knew that there was no use complaining. He just looked out the window at the hilly scenery. They passed a farmer herding goats along the road. Aldo's mother waved, and the man called back, "Grazia, welcome home!"

As soon as *Nonno* and *Nonna* heard a car pulling up to their house, they came out to greet Aldo and his parents with hugs and kisses.

"It took you a long time to get here!" *Nonno* said as he hugged Aldo. "There was a traffic jam getting out of Florence," *Mama* replied. "It's not like here, where there are hardly any cars on the road."

Aldo hadn't visited his grandparents' home in three years, since he was nine years old. It was much smaller than he remembered — and there was still no TV.

*(above) Aldo enjoys a **gelato** on the way to his grandparents' home.*

*(top) A dirt road winds through the grassy hills on the way to **Nonna and Nonno's** village.*

Just then Isabella came in, carrying groceries from the *piazza* shops. Aldo was surprised to see his fourteen-year-old cousin. "*Ciao*, Isabella," he called out.

"*Ciao*, Aldo," she answered. "Come help me with these bags."

"Isabella came from Rome for some rest after her exams," *Nonna* said. She took Isabella's hand and squeezed it. "She's nervous because she doesn't know how she did."

"Aldo, how was school this year?" Isabella asked, changing the subject. She didn't want to talk about the exams she had to write before entering senior high school.

"We went on a field trip to Pisa for three days," Aldo replied. "It was great seeing the Leaning Tower again."

"Next year, your class should come to Rome to visit the ancient ruins," Isabella suggested.

"Ah, it makes me so sad," *Nonna* interrupted. "My Aldo in Florence, my Isabella in Rome. Both so far away."

"Then, come live with us!" *Babbo* insisted.

"No, the countryside is too much in our bones," *Nonna* said. "Everyone in the village is like family. We grew up with them, we survived the war together, and we still see them every day."

Soon, the family was enjoying the large lunch that *Nonna* had made. Everyone had fresh pasta and vegetables, bread with olive oil, and wine. For dessert, they had *espresso* and sweets. After the table was cleared, they all walked to the *piazza*. Every family was out for a *passegiata*.

"It's so relaxing here," Isabella said as they sat around the fountain.

"But there's nothing to do," Aldo complained. "No TV, no movie theater."

Isabella laughed. "I know plenty of games we can play — like *briscola*."

"But we don't have any cards," Aldo frowned.

"Then, put out your fist."

Aldo had forgotten about *morra*. Faster and faster, they stuck out their fingers and called numbers until they were shouting and laughing. "If you're not careful, Aldo, you might actually start having a good time," *Mama* teased.

Aldo knew Isabella and his parents were right. It didn't matter that the city was so far away. It was fun to be with his family. He finally relaxed and looked forward to the rest of his visit.

Nonna *sprinkles grated Parmesan cheese over the fresh pasta and homemade tomato sauce that she prepared for lunch.*

Glossary

accessories Items that complement clothing, such as jewelry, hats, and shoes.

allies Nations united by an agreement to help one another, especially in times in war

ancestor A person from whom one is descended

baptism A Christian ceremony during which a person is dipped or washed in water as a sign of washing away sin

bribe Money or other gift given to someone so that he or she will commit a dishonest or illegal act that benefits the giver

cathedral A large church

confirmation A Christian ceremony in which a person renews his or her faith and is given full membership in the Church

corruption Dishonesty, often in politics or business

culture The customs, beliefs, and arts of a distinct group of people

dam A wall built across a body of water to control the flow of water

descendant A person who can trace his or her family roots to a certain family or group

emperor The ruler of a country or group of countries

empire A group of countries or territories with the same ruler or government

execute To put to death

first communion A Christian ceremony in which a person receives holy bread and wine for the first time

immigrant A person who settles in another country

livestock Farm animals

medieval Belonging to the period of history from about 500 A.D. to 1500 A.D., known as the Middle Ages

merchant A person who buys and sells goods

nobility People born into a high social class

patriotic Full of love for one's country

piazza A public square in an Italian town

prophet A person who is believed to speak on behalf of a god

rebellion An uprising against a government

refugee A person who leaves his or her home or country because of danger

reservoir A place for storing water

revolution The overthrow of a government

suburb A residential area outside a city

trade An occupation, usually involving a craft or skill

 # Index

1 2 3 4 5 6 7 8 9 0 Printed in the USA 0 9 8 7 6 5 4 3 2 1

Italian students on a school trip to Venice.

A police officer has found a scooter parked in the wrong spot.

Italians love their dogs

An Italian Family

Family and work photos of Patrisio (Patrick) Berengo and Giselle Pugliese. They live in an apartment in Mestre, near Venice. They have two children, Giacomo, who is two years old, and Mariasole, who is one. Patrisio is the president of a company that makes machinery parts. Giselle is in charge of arranging special events at the Venice Holiday Inn. Giselle is shown with the hotel manager and her co-workers.